# Naming Colors

These are the ancestors of a few English color words:

Rouge—French, Red

Rubi—Middle French, Ruby

Rosso—Italian, Red

Endego—Portuguese, Indigo

Rād—Old Frisian, Red

Blāo—Old High Germanic, Blue

Cherise—Norman French, Cherry

Līlak—Persian, Lilac

Za'farān—Arabic, Saffron

Améthystos—Greek, Amethyst

Brūn—Anglo-Saxon, Brown

Piedra de ijada—means "colic stone" in Spanish.

Kraanbere—means "crane berry" in Low German,

Hwīt—Old English, White

Ruber—Latin, Red

Gruoni—Old High German, Green

Blar—Old Icelandic, Blue

Nāraṅja—Sanskrit, Orange

# Naming Colors

## ARIANE DEWEY

HarperCollins*Publishers*

Sappīr—Hebrew, Sapphire

Persicum mālum—means "Persian apple" in Latin, Peach

Jade was thought to prevent colic, a painful stomach ache.

Bhru—Aryan, beaver, Brown

Cranberry

ashes of roses     azure     butterscotch

café au lait

carmine

This book is dedicated to a lot of colorful women.
My grandmother who hated blue and loved chartreuse, my mother who
taught me how to see and appreciate color, my sister Suki with whom I share
purple, my godmother Suzie, Mrs. Noling, Madame Wadlow, and supportive
Judy, Julie, Sabine, Sheila, Helen, and Harrie.

chamois

eggshell     flamingo pink     gage green     glacier blue

Dewey red     mulberry     oxblood

Naming Colors
Copyright © 1995 by Ariane Dewey
All rights reserved. No part of this book may be used or reproduced in any manner whatsoever without
written permission except in the case of brief quotations embodied in critical articles and reviews.
Printed in Mexico. For information address HarperCollins Children's Books, a division of
HarperCollins Publishers, 10 East 53rd Street, New York, NY 10022.

Library of Congress Cataloging-in-Publication Data
Dewey, Ariane.
    Naming colors / by Ariane Dewey.
        p.      cm.
    Includes index.
    Summary: Describes how various colors came to have their specific names in English.
    ISBN 0-06-021291-8. — ISBN 0-06-021292-6 (lib. bdg.)
    1. Colors—Nomenclature—Juvenile literature.   [1. Color.   2. English language—Etymology.]
    1. Title.
    QC495.5.D5   1995                                                                93-2635
    535.6'014—dc20                                                                       CIP
                                                                                          AC

Typography by Tom Starace
1   2   3   4   5   6   7   8   9   10
❖
First Edition

sea-foam green

viridian

teal     U.N. blue     Vandyke Brown

hyacinth    iceberg green         Kelly green         mauve

harvest gold                                                          livid

                                                                 midnight blue

# AUTHOR'S NOTE

*Color is my passion. I became fascinated with how we describe
the multitude of colors we see. This is a personal collection of
colors, joyfully selected. I have chosen what are, for me, the most
intriguing, quirky, or amusing stories. There are certainly others.
More space is given to alabaster than to pink because its history is
more interesting. Pink was named after the flower by that name.*

*Root words have not always been included in the text, as this is
not a linguistic tome. They can be found, among other places, in:*
The American Heritage Dictionary of the English Language, *2nd
College Edition.* The Barnhart Dictionary of Etymology, *Robert K.
Barnhart, editor.* Webster's Word Histories, *by Merriam-Webster
Inc.*

*The rest of my bibliography is too extensive to include here, but
particularly helpful were:* Basic Color Terms: Their Universality
and Evolution, *by Brent Berlin and Paul Kay.* Color: A Survey in
Words and Pictures from Ancient Mysticism to Modern Science, *by
Faber Birren.* A Dictionary of Color, *by A. Maerz and M. Rea Pasul.*
Color, *edited by Helen Varley. I read many, some extremely funny,
books on curious English word histories.*

*I love libraries, and I'd like to thank the ones where I did my
research: The Society Library, The New York Public Library at 42nd
Street, and the Cold Spring Harbor Library. And thanks to my ever-
patient editor, Katherine Brown Tegen.*

*A.D.*

persimmon                                                        zest pink

platinum                                                    Williamsburg blue

quince        roan    Rubens red        sanguine                         5

# BEGINNING WITH WORDS

There are millions of colors that can be seen by the human eye. This is the story of how people named some of the colors that they saw. It is a story that comes out of the histories of all the people on Earth. The origins of the names of colors are as varied as the stories of different people and the thousands of languages they speak.

No one knows exactly when or where language first evolved. Nor do we know why early people agreed on a certain combination of sounds to represent an event, an object, or a color; but we can trace many words back to very ancient times.

About 6000 years ago Neolithic people living in central Eurasia spoke a language we call Indo-European. Today, almost half the people in the world speak languages descended from this mother tongue. As Indo-European tribes scattered across the continents, they carried their language with them. More words were added, other words were lost. Pronunciation changed. People met and taught each other new words. And so the many languages of our world grew and flourished.

# THE GROWTH OF ENGLISH

Long ago a people called the Celts lived in what is now England. In A.D. 43 they were invaded by the Romans, who named the land Britannia. Although the Romans remained in Britannia for four hundred years, their language, Latin, was little used by the native people. The Celts continued to speak Celtic among themselves.

After the Romans left, England was repeatedly overrun by tribes from northern Europe, including the Angles and the Saxons. The languages of these tribes blended with Celtic, and about 1500 years ago, English began to emerge as a separate language.

English continued to take words from successive invaders, especially the Norman French, who came in 1066. Travelers brought more words from faraway lands. Some of the languages that contributed words to English are Sanskrit, Greek, Latin, Celtic, Saxon, Italian, French, Spanish, Icelandic, and Danish. English has also taken words from Mandarin Chinese, Hebrew, Arabic, and Nahuatl, the language of the Aztecs, as well as other Native American languages. The list goes on and on.

# NAMING THE BASIC COLORS

Only a small number of the colors we see have been named. Color is hard to describe, because it is always part of something else. For more than 2000 years philosophers and scientists have tried to explain the qualities of color.

Prehistoric people probably named the common things around them first: sun, sky, grass. Later, they gave names to colors to help them describe these things: yellow sun, blue sky, green grass.

From earliest times people have used colors as symbols for important aspects of their lives: yellow for warmth, goodness, or creation; red for aggression or life; green for fertility, wisdom, or youth. Colors became magical representatives of these things in rituals. Black and white have often represented death and rebirth. Many societies associated colors, though not necessarily the same ones, with the directions—north, south, east, and west—and with fire, air, water, and earth.

There appears to be an order in which colors are named as languages grow. The order is: ● black, ○ white, ● red, ○ yellow, ● green (or green, yellow), ● blue, and then ● brown, ● purple, ○ pink, ● orange, and ○ grey, although many languages do not have words for all these colors.

The words for BLACK and WHITE are the first two color-related terms found in all languages. They are named together; it seems that no language has only one color word. Black and white were used to describe darkness and lightness. Black is the absence of light, while white reflects light.

The origin of the English word black probably comes from an Indo-European root meaning "burnt." In Old English the word was *blæc*. White goes back to an Indo-European root that meant "shining brightness." The Old English color word was *hwīt*.

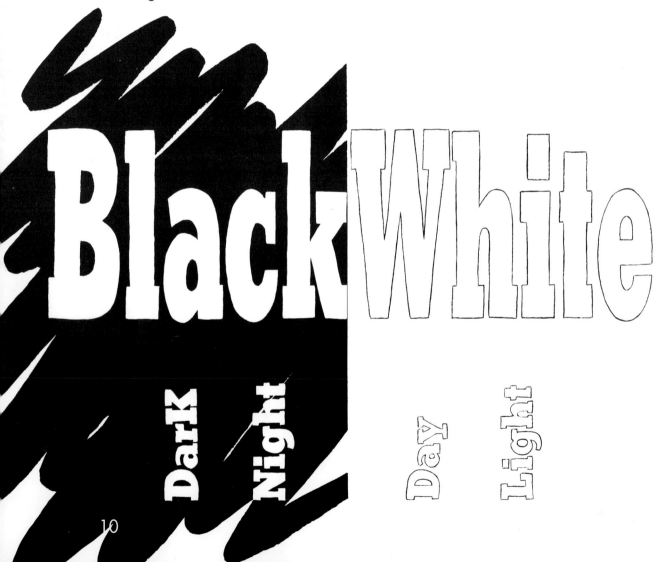

RED, the color of blood, has been a symbol of life from earliest times. Prehistoric men and women used flaming red fires to cook, to scare away wild animals, and to stay warm. For these reasons, red was very important. So after black and white, red was the next color to be named. The English color word red can be traced back through Old English, Latin, and Sanskrit to its Indo-European roots.

Our eyes see red as the strongest color, making red objects stand out and appear to be closer than objects of other colors. Because red is somewhat rare in nature, it catches our eye and gets a reaction. This is why we use red for danger signs.

11

Yellow

Green

Blue

YELLOW was associated with gold and with the sun, the brightest thing in our world. Farmers have always depended upon warm sunlight to make their crops grow. Yellow became a symbol of warmth and prosperity.

The words grass, GREEN, and grow all come from a single Indo-European root. The ancient Egyptians described time as "the everlasting green one." This expression connected the idea of time with the seasonal cycle of growth and death, planting and harvesting. Green was an important color because it represented the growth of plants that provided food for people and the animals they hunted.

The history of BLUE is not as clear as those of the other basic colors. Color names sometimes shifted from one color to another. The root words of blue meant "brightness" in Sanskrit, "white" in Greek, "yellow" in Latin, and "the color of a black-and-blue bruise" in Old Icelandic. The current English spelling of blue did not come into regular use until the 1700s.

These basic colors, BLACK, WHITE, RED, YELLOW, GREEN, and BLUE, helped people to identify or pick out things in groups, such as yellow flowers, black bears, or red rocks. Changes in the color of an object also tell us about its condition. Green berries aren't ready to eat, but when they turn red or black or blue, they are ripe and sweet. Some metals turn red or white when they are extremely hot. Color words help us describe these changes.

Many objects, however, cannot be accurately described by using only one of the basic color words. Adding adjectives, to make phrases like dark blue or light green, made it possible to describe a wider range of colors. Or to be more precise, colors could be combined into phrases like blue-green or yellowish-green. But more words were still needed to describe the abundance of colors that people saw around them. The easiest and most common way to name a color was to give it the name of something it resembled, like SKY BLUE. Saying ORANGE for the color of that fruit, for example, was easier and clearer than saying reddish-yellow.

People have expressed themselves with color from the earliest times. Around 30,000 B.C., Stone Age painters began covering cave walls with red, yellow, and black animals and people. Ever since then, artists have been grinding earth, stones, and plants into powders to use for colors. These powders, or pigments, were mixed with liquid such as water, oil, gum, or egg whites to make paint. Many color names come from the names of these pigments.

Weavers made dyes, liquid colors in which materials can be soaked, to color thread or whole cloth. Many of these colors took the names of the plants or minerals from which they were made.

Today, chemical dyes, which are more permanent and cheaper to mass produce than natural dyes, are used commercially. And because manufacturers of paints, cosmetics, fabrics, and even automobiles want their products to seem unique and chic, they invent color names like AUTUMN GOLD, DUSTY ROSE, and SUGARED GRAPEFRUIT. One intense, trendy, fashion color has been known as SHOCKING PINK, HOT PINK, and ELECTRIC PINK.

Our lives are filled with bright and beautiful fruits, vegetables, flowers, plants, jewels, rocks, animals, places, and fabrics. All of these have been used to help people name different colors.

# COLORS FROM THE GARDEN

The many colors of fruits and vegetables made them a perfect source for color names.

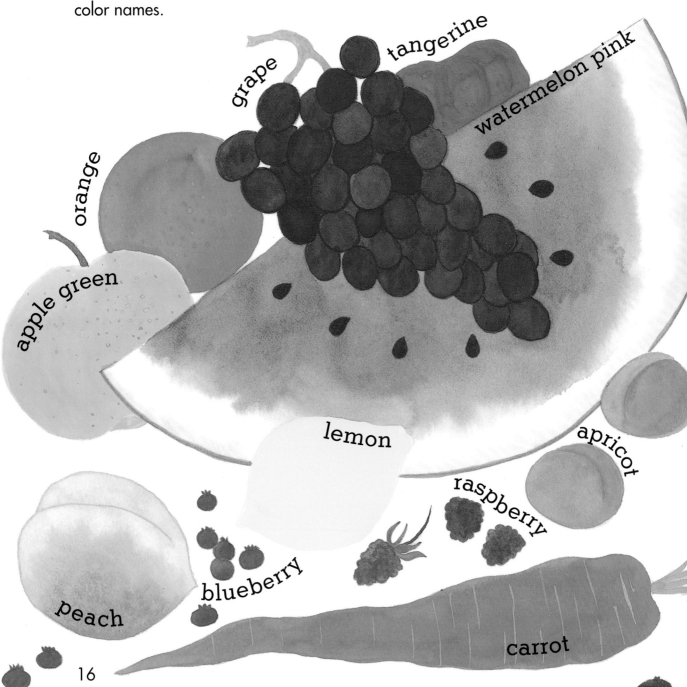

grape

tangerine

watermelon pink

orange

apple green

lemon

apricot

raspberry

peach

blueberry

carrot

16

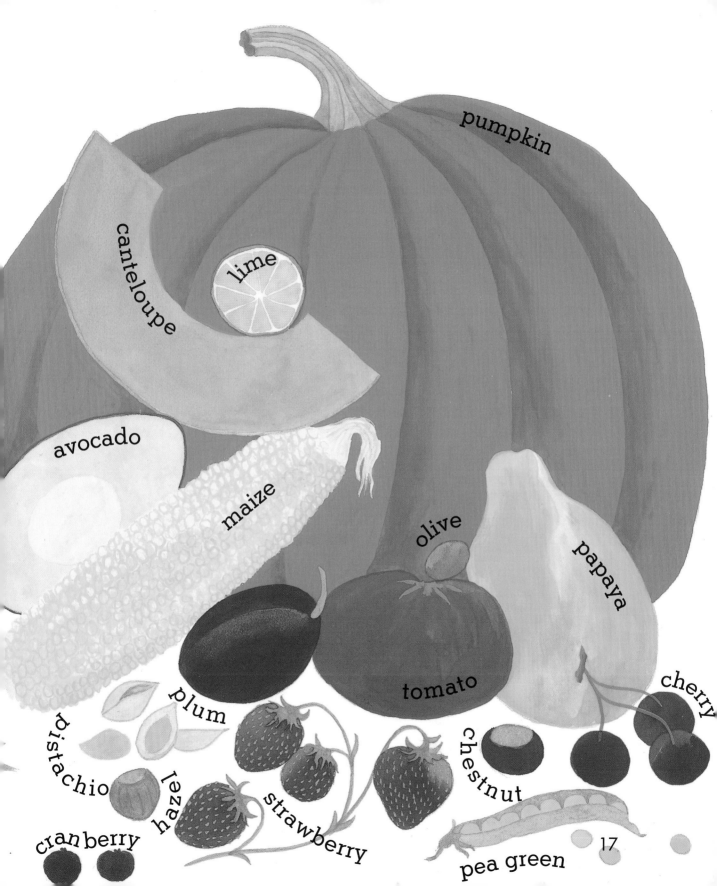

pumpkin

canteloupe

lime

avocado

maize

olive

papaya

plum

tomato

cherry

pistachio

chestnut

hazel

strawberry

cranberry

pea green

17

Some of these names have interesting histories. Orange, maize, and grape are good examples. Oranges were brought to Europe from the Middle East, along with their Arabic name, *nāranj*. The spelling changed to *naranja* in Spanish and *orange* in French. Before the fruit arrived in Europe, there was no word for this color. Now the word ORANGE describes any object with that warm, cheery color.

In 1492 Columbus's crew found the native people on the island now called Cuba growing a grain called *mahiz*. This grain was tender and delicious. The native people, whom Columbus mistakenly called Indians, dried the grain and then ground it into flour. Columbus took some of the seeds home to Spain. The plant was so hardy that it was soon growing in much of Europe. It had been growing wild in the Americas for some 80,000 years. The English call it maize after the Indian word. In the United States it is called corn, a word that means wheat or grain in England. The color MAIZE is corn color.

Curious stories, little-known facts, and strange incidents explain how other colors were named for fruits and vegetables. One example is the color GRAPE. The word *grape* in Old French referred to the hook that was used to pluck the fruit from the vines. The meaning of the word *grape* slowly shifted from the hook to the fruit. From there, the word *grape* also came to mean the color of the dark, purple-red fruit. The English language adopted the French word *grape*.

# ROSE IS A ROSE IS A ROSE

Flowers bloom in every brilliant color imaginable. So it is surprising that more colors do not have flower names. Odd too is the fact that nearly all the color names come from pink or purple flowers.

FUCHSIA is a violent pinky-purple color. The unusual name fuchsia was given to a flowering shrub in honor of the sixteenth-century botanist Leonard Fuchs. The startling color fuchsia got its name from the flowers of this plant.

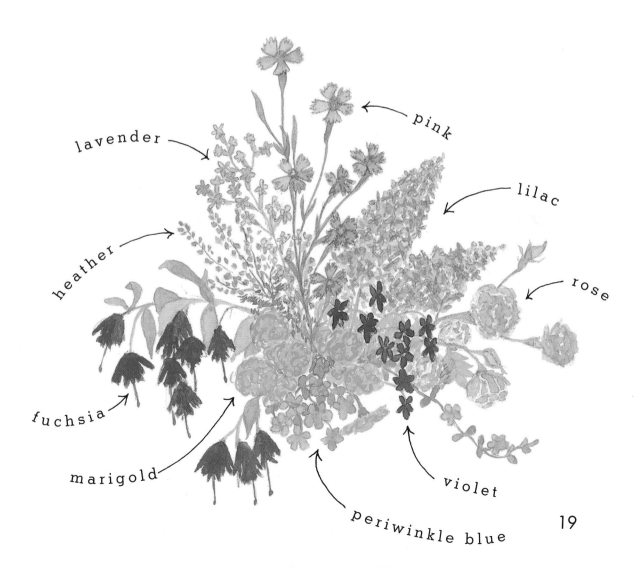

lavender

pink

lilac

heather

rose

fuchsia

marigold

violet

periwinkle blue

The landscape is rich in color names. The Old English word for GRASS GREEN, *græsgrœ̄ni*, appeared over 1300 years ago, making it one of the earliest color words in English. CYPRESS GREEN is the color of that evergreen tree's needles.

The color TAN probably comes from a Celtic word for oak tree. Tan is the color of leather. Rawhide was soaked with the crushed bark of the oak tree, which contains an acid called tannin, to preserve the hide by turning it into leather. The process is called tanning.

# SPICY COLORS

Food spoils quickly in warm weather when there is no place to keep it cool. The household electric refrigerator is a 20th-century invention. Before that time, pungent spices were used to obscure the rotten taste and odor of foul meat and vegetables. In medieval Europe, pepper, nutmeg, saffron, cinnamon, and cloves were as precious as gold.

During the 15th, 16th, and 17th centuries, the demand for spices was so great that traders traveled the world to obtain them. Gold, precious stones, silks, carpets, and spices were all to be found in the Far East. Columbus was looking for a direct route from Europe, across the Atlantic Ocean to the riches of the East, when he landed on an island in the Bahamas by mistake.

For centuries caravans crossed Asia and ships sailed around Africa, bringing spices to Europe. The spice trade thrived, supplying the world's markets. The delicious colors of ground spices made them an obvious source of color names.

DRIED NUTMEG

MINT TEA
MINT TEA
MINT TEA
MINT TEA
MINT TEA
MINT TEA
MINT TEA
MINT TEA
MINT TEA
MINT TEA
MINT TEA
MINT TEA
MINT TEA
MINT TEA

DRIED MINT

CINNAMON

MINT GREEN

NUTMEG,
ground seeds of the
evergreen nutmeg tree
from the Molucca
Islands of Indonesia.

MINT GREEN,
fresh or dried
leaves of mint
plants.

MINT

CINNAMON,
dried inner
bark of an
evergreen tree
native to
Sri Lanka.

PEPPERS

PAPRIKA,
dried and powdered
sweet red peppers
from Hungary.

SAGE, fresh or dried leaves of sage plants.

SAGE SAGE
SAGE SAGE SAGE
SAGE SAGE SAGE SAGE

VANILLA, seed pods of tropical American orchids called vanilla.

The color Vanilla is off white, like vanilla flavored ice cream, even though Vanilla beans are blackish-brown.

GROUND GINGER

CANDIED GINGER

MUSTARD MUSTARD

MUSTARD SEEDS

GINGER, fresh or dried powdered root of the Asian ginger plant.

MUSTARD, powdered seeds of mustard plants native to Eurasia.

SAFFRON, dried stigmas of the crocus flower.

# JEWEL-LIKE COLORS

Since prehistoric times people have drilled holes in colorful stones, strung these beads together, and worn them around their necks. Ever since, men and women have delighted in decorating themselves with jewels.

Amber is not really a stone, but it looks like one. It has been highly valued since the Stone Age, when people were already using it to decorate themselves. Amber seemed magical because it becomes electrically charged when rubbed.

Amber is fossilized tree sap. Bugs have been found caught in the sticky resin, which took millions of years to harden. Beetles, ants, flies, and even small tree toads have been perfectly preserved in amber. Jewelers set these golden-yellow stones in elegant rings and necklaces.

The English word amber was borrowed from Old French *ambre*, meaning a greyish substance, called ambergris in English, that is produced by whales. The French word comes from Medieval Latin *ambar*, from Arabic *'anbar*. In England AMBER was being used as a color name by 1500.

ruby

amethyst

lapis lazuli

gold

jet

aquamarine

pearl

jade

silver

turquoise

emerald

sapphire

topaz

25

Bast

In ancient times, the Egyptians venerated all cats to honor the cat goddess, Bast. When cats died, they were carefully preserved as mummies and buried in her temple in coffins made of gypsum. This fine, pale, translucent stone was named *a-la-baste* in her honor. The English word ALABASTER means both the stone and its pale-yellowish color.

alabaster

Precious stones have always been prized for their sparkling colors, so naturally they are sources of color names. Mysterious myths and romantic tales hover around these gems.

TOPAZ comes from the Greek *topazos*, a word of uncertain meaning, which possibly comes from *topazein*, "to guess." One fanciful story claims the traders or pirates who brought the semiprecious stone to Greece would not reveal its origin. The Greeks imagined that it came from a mysterious island shrouded in fog. They could only guess its location.

Another Greek legend tells of Amethyst, a lovely nymph who implored the goddess Artemis to protect her from the advances of the wine god Dionysus. So Artemis changed Amethyst into a gemstone. And Dionysus turned the stone the color of wine in memory of his lost love. The color AMETHYST comes from this precious stone. The original Greek word *améthystos* means "something that prevents drunkenness." The ancient Greeks believed that anyone who wore an amethyst could not get drunk.

# COLORS FROM THE EARTH

Seemingly useless sticky lumps, smelly crystals, and muddy earth have also contributed color names. The color OCHER is made from a yellowish clay, also called ocher, and is one of the oldest pigments known. SLATE is the color and the name of a rock that cracks into thin layers. These were the original blackboards, as they provided a hard, flat surface to write on.

*Sulpur* is the Latin word for a bright-yellow element found naturally in crystals, lumps, or powder. An acid-yellow pigment is made from SULPHUR. Because sulphur burns, it is also called brimstone, or burn-stone, as in "hellfire and brimstone." Burning sulphur smells like rotten eggs. People said a stink so terrible must come straight from hell!

The color PITCH BLACK refers to tar derived from wood, coal, or oil. The phrase "black as *pych*," an old spelling for pitch, was recorded more than 600 years ago in England.

Even rocks have amusing stories to tell. COBALT BLUE comes from the German word *Kobold*, a mischievous household spirit. Miners blamed this tricky gnome for mishaps in the mine. They also accused the malicious goblin of stealing precious silver and leaving behind worthless rock that looked as though it contained metal but didn't. They mockingly called the false ore *Kobold*. The name stuck even when the stone was found to be useful as, among other things, a blue pigment.

29

# COLORS FROM EVERY LIVING THING

An amazing variety of animals has influenced color names. Some animal names, such as CORAL, FAWN, and RAVEN, became color words. We also have CAMEL COLOR, DOVE GREY, IVORY, MOUSE GREY, PEACOCK BLUE, PEARL GREY, and ROBIN'S-EGG BLUE. BROWN, bear, and beaver all come from the same Indo-European root, which probably referred to the color of the fur of bears and beavers. BUFF is the color of the soft leather made from buffalo hide. PUCE is the color of a flea's tummy, from the Latin word for flea, *pulex*. TAUPE means "mole" in French.

Other creatures have lent their influence indirectly. There is a mussel found only in the Mediterranean Sea near Tyre. The Greeks called it *porphyros*. These shellfish produce tiny drops of liquid, which were used to prepare a wonderful dye. In Latin the mussel, its dye, and cloth colored with this dye were called *purpura*. As many as 10,000 shellfish were needed to fill one tiny pot with dye. So rare and expensive was this dye that only emperors and kings could afford to color their robes with it. This lush color is called PURPLE in English, sometimes even ROYAL PURPLE.

There is no color named cuttlefish, but this strange creature also produces a dye. *Sépíā* is the Greek word for the brown fluid the  cuttlefish squirts at its enemies. The Romans used it in making ink. Later, SEPIA came to mean the color of this ink.

Worms are responsible for three color names, SCARLET, CRIMSON, and VERMILION. The dried body or the fluid of the heart-shaped kermes worm was used to make a rich red dye. *Krimi-s*, the Sanskrit word for "worm," passed into Persian, Arabic, Latin, and Old Spanish. Along the way the meaning changed from the worm to the color. The word crimson means a brilliant red in English.

In 1148 the French Crusaders brought home magnificent cloth from the Holy Land. It had been woven and colored, with kermes dye, in Persia. There the fabric was called *siqillāt*, the source, via Latin and French, of the English color word scarlet.

The color word vermilion also comes from a worm, a maggot actually, called the cochineal, which is native to Mexico and was used to make dye. *Vermiculus* means "little worm, vermin, or crawling insect" in Latin.

canary yellow

Dogs influenced a color name in a roundabout way. CANARY YELLOW comes from the Latin word *canis*, "dog." In 40 B.C. King Juba of Numidia, an ancient land in northwest Africa, found some islands in the Atlantic. He reported that a great number of wild dogs lived there. Based on this information, the Romans later named the islands *Canāriae Īnsulae*, Dog Islands. When the Spanish saw the little yellow songbirds that live there, they named them *canarias* after the islands. The color canary yellow was named after the birds.

# COLORFUL PLACES

Another island that is related to color names is Cyprus. In Roman times the island was famous for its copper mines. The Latin word for copper meant "a metal coming from Cyprus." Later, the reddish-gold color of this metal was also called by the same name. In English we call the metal and the color COPPER.

Ancient people created the first alloy by combining copper and tin. The resulting metal and its color may take their name, BRONZE, from the Roman port city of Brundisium, where metal of particularly high quality was produced.

The tragedy of another Roman city preserved a brilliant color for us. The eruption of Mount Vesuvius in A.D. 79 buried the city of Pompeii in ashes. Centuries later, archaeologists digging at the site discovered wonderful murals whose predominant color was a uniquely rich red. They called it POMPEIAN RED.

Over the ages traveling traders have brought us many words. PEACH comes from the Greek and Latin words for "Persian apple." This was shortened to peche in French and peach in English. The fruit actually came from China, a place too distant for Europeans to imagine. So the peach was named after Persia, the country through which it had come from the faraway East. By the same reasoning,

TURQUOISE means comes from Turkey through Turkey from Turkestan. Turkish, not because the stone but because it was brought west

Lapis lazuli, a rare stone brought from Persia, was ground fine to make a deep-blue pigment. This color was called ULTRAMARINE, a Latin word meaning "beyond the sea," because that's where it came from. AQUAMARINE comes from the Latin word meaning "seawater." Another blue color, INDIGO, comes from a Greek word literally meaning "stuff that comes from beyond the Indus River," in India. Blue dye is extracted from the leaves of a plant; indigo is the name of the plant, the dye, and the color. Blue jeans are the color i n d i g o, though they are now dyed with chemicals.

As more and more exotic fruits appeared in Europe, they and their colors continued to be named for their places of origin. DAMSON is a plum from Damascus, the TANGERINE comes from Tanger, and a kind of coffee was named mocha after the port in Yemen from which it was shipped. Now MOCHA often means a mixture of coffee and hot chocolate, or the color of this drink.

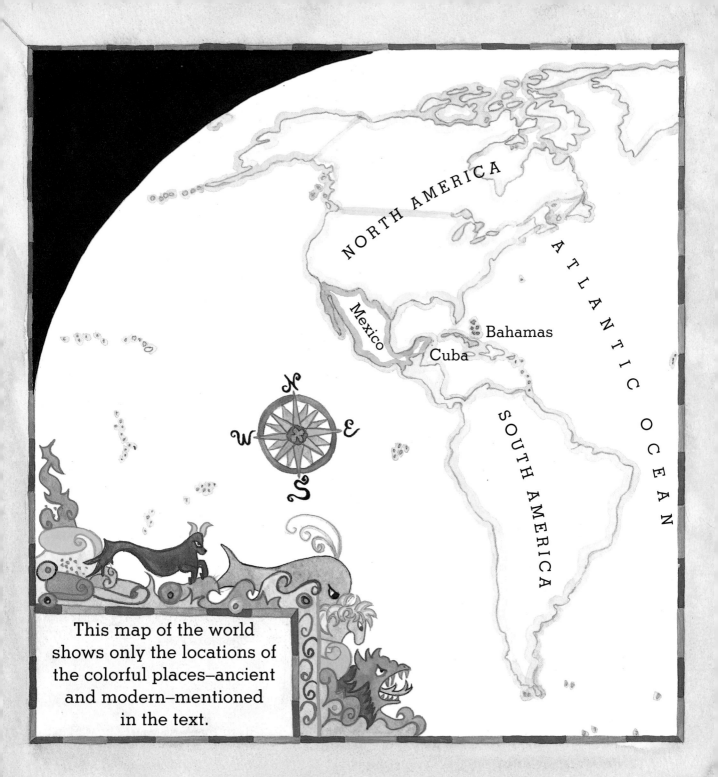

NORTH AMERICA

ATLANTIC OCEAN

Mexico

Bahamas

Cuba

SOUTH AMERICA

N
W E
S

This map of the world shows only the locations of the colorful places—ancient and modern—mentioned in the text.

Iceland

England

E U R O P E

A S I A

Venice

Turkestan

Greece

Turkey

China

Mediterranean

Canary
Islands

Tanger

Sea

Cyprus

Damascus

Indus River

Numidia

Tyre

Persia

India

Egypt

A F R I C A

Nile River

Yemen

Mocha

Indonesia

Moluccas

Wine has long been a popular drink. A 3500-year-old Egyptian mural shows people stomping on grapes to prepare wine. There are hieroglyphs for the growing vine and for the wine press. The deep red-purple color of some wines is known as WINE RED. But particular wines have also given their names to colors. BORDEAUX and BURGUNDY are French wines, the regions in which the wines are produced, and the colors of these wines.

Bordeaux

Burgundy

The monks of the Carthusian order used herbs to make a yellow-green medicinal brandy, which they named after their monastery, La Grande Chartreuse. The color of the brandy was so striking that CHARTREUSE became a color name.

The clay around the Italian city of SIENNA made excellent pigment. It is used raw to make yellowish-brown or burned for reddish-brown. These colors are called RAW SIENNA and BURNT SIENNA. The brown earth of Umbria, a region of central Italy, was also made into the pigments RAW UMBER and BURNT UMBER. The area was named for a tribe, the Umbri, who lived there. The Renaissance painters of Venice had a favorite shade of red that they used so often, it came to be known as VENETIAN RED.

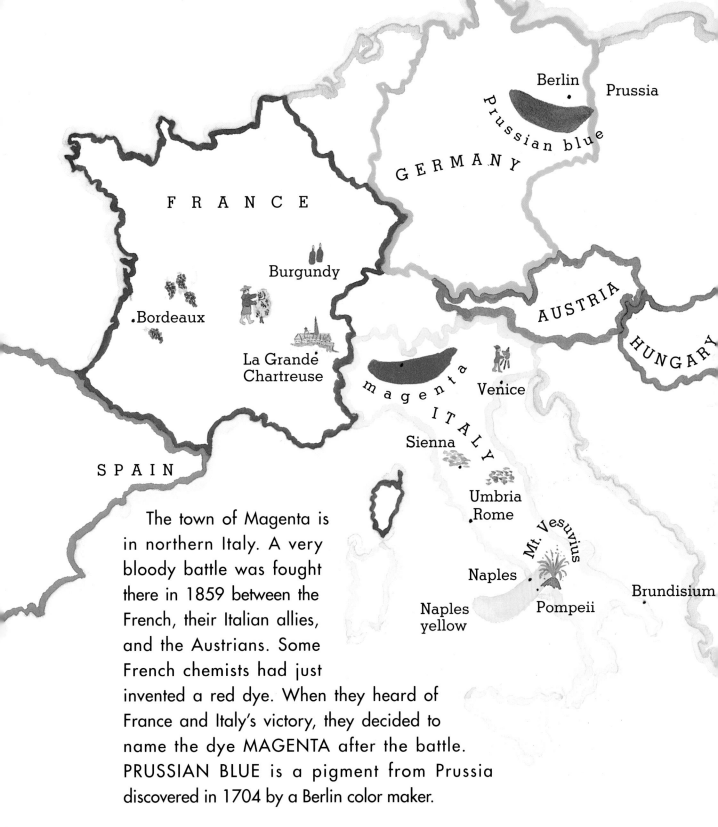

Berlin
Prussia

*Prussian blue*

G E R M A N Y

F R A N C E

Burgundy

.Bordeaux

La Grandé
Chartreuse

AUSTRIA

HUNGARY

*magenta*

Venice

I T A L Y

Sienna

Umbria
Rome

Naples

Mt. Vesuvius

Pompeii

Brundisium

Naples
yellow

S P A I N

The town of Magenta is
in northern Italy. A very
bloody battle was fought
there in 1859 between the
French, their Italian allies,
and the Austrians. Some
French chemists had just
invented a red dye. When they heard of
France and Italy's victory, they decided to
name the dye MAGENTA after the battle.
PRUSSIAN BLUE is a pigment from Prussia
discovered in 1704 by a Berlin color maker.

39

# COLORS TO EAT

Besides vegetables, fruits, herbs, and spices, there are many colorful raw and prepared foods. One of the most delicious is chocolate. Hernando Cortés, the Spanish conqueror, noticed that the Aztec nobles of Mexico enjoyed a cold drink made from ground cacao beans flavored with wild honey, vanilla pods, and spicy hot peppers. It was called *chocolatl*, which meant literally "bitter water."

The Aztecs considered cacao beans to be so precious that they used them for money. The drink was extremely expensive and was reserved for the aristocracy. Montezuma, the Aztec ruler, drank from cups of pure gold. Cortés introduced the drink to Spain, where it was served hot and sweetened with sugar. It was the deep-brown color we call CHOCOLATE.

chocolate

# COLORS TO WEAR

When cloth was still being woven by hand, weavers had many words for the types of cloth they produced. BEIGE and ECRU, fun words to say, come from the French names for the colors of natural undyed wool or cotton. A rough brownish-red homespun cloth was called *rousset* in French. In English, RUSSET came to mean the color only. English borrowed all these color names.

Sometimes the color of a person's clothes tells us about him or her. Mothers got tired of being asked, "Is it a boy or a girl?" So they dressed their infants in BABY BLUE or BABY PINK. A little girl who hates pink could have a problem!

Clothes may not make the man, but they sometimes tell us who he is. Cardinals of the Roman Catholic Church can be distinguished by the red robes they wear. The color CARDINAL RED is taken from the priests' robes. The cardinal bird was named after the color.

Uniforms are also worn for identification. The English army in India wore red jackets, which made the soldiers easy targets. During an uprising in 1857, they began wearing uniforms made from an earth-colored cotton called *khaki*, the Urdu word for "dust." The new uniforms blended into the landscape, helping to protect the soldiers from snipers. Army uniforms have been KHAKI colored ever since. ARMY DRAB, a muddier version of the same color, also provides excellent camouflage. One of the most common colors for clothes is NAVY BLUE, like sailors' uniforms.

cardinal red

khaki

army drab

navy blue

# OLD AND NEW COLORS

Words for colors keep changing. Old words are dropped and new words are created. For example, since the invention of electricity, oil and kerosene lamps do not light every home. With no smoky lamps to clean, there is no soot with which to make the pigment LAMPBLACK. Nor is SNUFF much used today. Few people are familiar with the color of this sneeze-producing powdered tobacco. And thus, color words drop from the language when they are no longer readily understood. New color descriptions are concocted, like BUBBLE-GUM PINK.

Today there are color charts and formulas for reproducing colors precisely by numbers. But it's not as much fun as saying something is the same color as a flea's belly or the result of a troublesome *Kobold*.

Lots and lots of other things have been used for color names. Here are a few of them. See if you can name some more. And have fun!

rust

battle ship grey

SKY BLUe

bottle green

smoke

brick red

flame red

fire engine red

sand

45

# INDEX

electric pink, 15

emerald, 25

**F**awn, 30

fire-engine red, 45

flame red, 11, 45

forest green, 20

fuchsia, 19

**G**inger, 23

gold, 25

grape, 16, 18

grass green, 9, 20

green, 3, 9, 12, 13

**H**azel, 16

heather, 19

honey, 40

hot pink, 15

**I**ndigo, 2, 35

ivory, 30

**J**ade, 2, 3, 25

jet black, 25

**K**haki, 43

**L**ampblack, 44

lavender, 19

lemon, 16

lilac, 2, 19

lime, 17

**M**agenta, 39

mahogany, 20

maize, 17, 18

marigold, 19

mint green, 22

mocha, 35, 37, 40

moss green, 20

mouse grey, 30

mushroom, 20

mustard, 23

**N**aples yellow, 39

navy blue, 43

Nile green, 37

nutmeg, 22

**O**atmeal, 40

ocher, 28

olive, 17

orange, 3, 9, 13, 16, 18

**P**apaya, 17

paprika, 22

peach, 3, 16, 34

peacock blue, 30

pea green, 17

pearl grey, 25, 30

periwinkle blue, 19

pink, 5, 9, 19

pistachio, 17

pitch black, 28

plum, 17

Pompeian red, 34

Prussian blue, 39

puce, 30

pumpkin, 17

purple, 9, 31

Raspberry, 16

raven, 30

raw sienna, 38

raw umber, 38

red, 2, 3, 9, 11, 13

robin's-egg blue, 30

rose, 19

ruby, 2, 25

russet, 42

rust, 44

Saffron, 2, 23

sage, 23

salmon, 40

sand, 45

sapphire blue, 3, 25

scarlet, 32

sepia, 32

shocking pink, 15

silver, 25, 29

sky blue, 9, 13, 45

slate grey, 28

smoke, 45

snuff, 44

strawberry, 17

sugared grapefruit, 15

sulphur, 28

Tan, 20

tangerine, 16, 35

taupe, 30

toast, 40

tomato red, 17

topaz, 25, 27

turquoise, 25, 35

Ultramarine, 35

Vanilla, 23

Venetian red, 38

vermilion, 32

violet, 19

Watermelon pink, 16

white, 3, 9, 10, 13

wine red, 38, 40

Yellow, 2, 9, 12, 13